The Young Children's Encyclopedia

Volume 4

Printed in the U.S.A.
Library of Congress Catalog Card Number: 87-80295
International Standard Book Number: 0-85229-478-6

Encyclopædia Britannica, Inc.

Chicago
Auckland   Rome
Geneva   Seoul
London   Sydney
Manila   Tokyo
Paris   Toronto

Table of Contents Volume 4

Here are more words beginning with "D" . . . *and* . . . **Here is where you may read about them**

Where Can I Get a Glass of Milk?

RAE IS VISITING HER AUNT AND UNCLE WHO LIVE ON A DAIRY FARM... A PLACE WHERE THERE ARE MANY, MANY COWS.

KITTY, THERE ISN'T ANY MILK. I WANT SOME, TOO.

WHERE CAN WE FIND SOME MILK--- I KNOW!

THE COW BARN IS A BIG MYSTERIOUS PLACE. HAY IS STORED IN THE HIGH HAYLOFT FOR THE COWS TO EAT IN THE WINTER.

MANY FARMERS MILK THEIR COWS BY MACHINE. THE MILK RUNS THROUGH PIPES TO THE COOLER.

ALL THE MILK IS GOING INTO THE MILKING MACHINE!

UNCLE BEN STILL MILKS OLD BESS BY HAND... THE OLD-FASHIONED WAY. COME ON, KITTEN. UNCLE BEN WILL GIVE US SOME MILK!

6

I COULD FILL YOUR MUG, RAE. BUT WHEN THE MILK FIRST COMES FROM THE COW, IT'S AS WARM AS THE COW'S BODY. I DON'T THINK YOU'D LIKE IT.

NO... I WANT A DRINK NOW, UNCLE BEN!

TO BE SURE THERE IS NO DIRT IN THE MILK, THE FARMER STRAINS IT AS IT GOES INTO THE COOLER.

A MILK FARM OUGHT TO BE THE BEST PLACE IN THE WORLD TO GET A DRINK OF MILK.

YOU'D THINK SO, WOULDN'T YOU? HEY, LOOK WHO'S COMING.

HERE'S THE DAIRY TRUCK TO TAKE THE MILK AWAY. HOW'D YOU LIKE TO RIDE WITH ME TO THE DAIRY?

ONLY IF I CAN FIND A DRINK OF MILK THERE.

DAIRIES BUY MILK FROM TESTED, HEALTHY COWS. THEN THE MILK FROM EACH FARM IS TESTED OFTEN TO MAKE SURE IT IS SAFE TO DRINK.

EVERYBODY OUT AT THE DAIRY.

NOW MAYBE I'LL GET A MUG OF MILK.

AFTER LEAVING THE FARM, THE MILK IS ALWAYS KEPT COVERED.

IT'S EVERYWHERE...IN THE TANKS, IN THE PIPES, AND IN THE MACHINES.

I'M TIRED OF WAITING. WHERE'S THE MILK, UNCLE BEN?

CREAM CAN BE SEPARATED FROM MILK TO MAKE COFFEE CREAM, WHIPPING CREAM, SOUR CREAM, CHEESE, ICE CREAM...OR IT CAN BE SWISHED BACK AND FORTH IN THE BUTTER-MAKING MACHINE TO MAKE BUTTER AND BUTTERMILK.

HERE'S THE CREAM SEPARATOR.

7

THIS HOMOGENIZER BREAKS UP THE BUTTERFAT IN THE MILK. IT MIXES THE CREAM WITH THE MILK.

I DON'T CARE ABOUT THE HOMOG-A-WHAT-CHAMACALLIT. I WANT A GLASS OF MILK.

AND THIS PASTEURIZER HEATS THE MILK JUST HOT ENOUGH TO KILL ANY BAD GERMS... RAE, WHERE ARE YOU GOING?

THE BOTTLING MACHINE WON'T FILL A CHIPPED MILK BOTTLE. THE MILK WILL GO INTO ONLY PERFECT BOTTLES... OR CARTONS.

BUT THAT MACHINE WON'T PUT MILK IN A MUG.

I WATCHED WHERE THE PIPES WENT AND I FOUND THE MILK. NOW STOP TEASING, UNCLE BEN. I WANT SOME.

THE CARTONS ARE SEALED QUICKLY SO THAT GERMS IN AIR DON'T GET INTO THE MILK.

THEN I'LL TAKE SOME MILK FROM A CARTON BEFORE THE TOP IS SEALED.

THE MACHINE HAS ALREADY SEALED THE CARTON. LET'S FOLLOW THE BASKETS AND SEE WHERE THEY GO.

HURRY, UNCLE BEN. SOME OF THE BASKETS ARE GOING THROUGH THOSE BIG DOORS. I'D BETTER FIND SOME MILK OUT THERE, TOO.

THE BASKETS CARRY BUTTER, COTTAGE CHEESE, WHIPPING CREAM... ALL THE GOOD THINGS THAT COME FROM THE COWS.

9

Flowers That Tell Fortunes

Daisies must love sunshine. They grow all over the world, in cold places and hot places, in fields and in gardens, wherever there is sunshine.

The common field daisy has a yellow center surrounded by white petals. But daisies come in many colors. Some are as tall as a man. Others are only a little higher than your shoe.

Every daisy "face" is made up of two main parts—the center, called the *disk,* and the outer petals, called the *rays.* People used to call a daisy the "day's eye" because they thought the yellow disk looked like a tiny sun in the middle of its petals, or rays. Actually, the disk is made up of many, many tiny flowers all squeezed together. Take one apart and you'll see!

Did you ever try to tell your fortune with a daisy? Sometimes a girl will pick one and take the petals off, one by one, saying, "He loves me . . . he loves me not. . . ." She hopes that when she picks off the last petal, she will be saying, "He loves me," for that will mean that her boyfriend loves her. Of course, a boy can pick the petals off in the same way, saying, "*She* loves me . . . she loves me not. . . ."

People used to think daisies were magic in many other ways, too. Some thought it was lucky to step on the first daisy they saw in the spring. (It wasn't lucky for the daisy!) Others believed that if daisies were floated in milk given to a puppy, the puppy would grow into a small, not a large, dog!

Not many people today believe in the old magic stories. But the daisies don't seem to care. They keep growing in the sunshine and nodding in the breeze.

If you liked this story,
look up Flowers *in Volume 6.*

11

The Artist Who Painted Dreams

Once there was a little boy in Spain who liked to wander over the rough hills and along the wild seashore. The strange shapes of shells and rocks and trees excited him. He carried a sketch pad and tried to draw nearly everything he saw.

When he was older, he went to art school. But he didn't want to paint the way everyone else did. He daydreamed and let his imagination suggest things to paint. He quarreled with his fellow students. He argued with his teachers. Finally he was expelled from school. But he kept on painting.

His name was Salvador Dali. He chose not to paint what most people call real things. Often he painted what he saw in dreams. In dreams anything can happen. Cats can have two tails. Buildings can be made of melting candy. Children can walk upside down on a ceiling.

© Philippe Halsman

12

Dali came to the United States and quickly became famous because his paintings showed such things as drooping watches. Some people laughed at first, saying that no watch ever looked that way. But Dali said that the watch had looked that way in his dream. He said that dreams are real to a person sleeping, so why shouldn't an artist paint what he sees in dreams?

More people began to agree. Dali is now one of the best-known painters in the world. Many artists now paint what they imagine or what they see in dreams.

Such artists are called *surrealists*.

*Other famous artists may be found
under* Gauguin *and* Goya *in Volume 7,*
Picasso *in Volume 12,*
and Van Gogh *in Volume 16.*

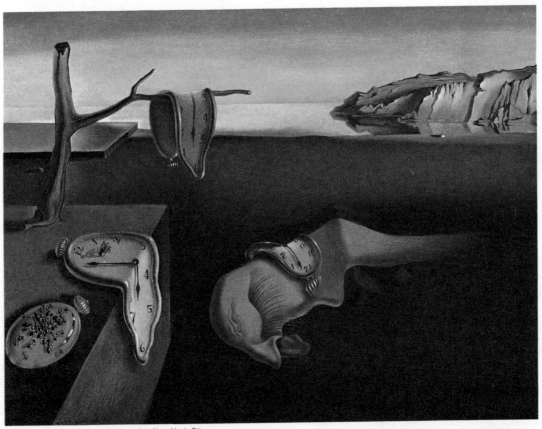

Courtesy of the Museum of Modern Art, New York City

The Wall That Holds Back Water

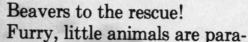

Beavers to the rescue!

Furry, little animals are parachuting into a faraway mountain forest. If the beavers work fast enough, they can prevent a flood.

This mountain stream looks calm and peaceful now. But soon spring rains and melting snow will make the stream swell with raging water. Unless these beavers get to work *fast*, the rushing floodwater will sweep down the mountainside, washing away trees and animals and even the houses that are in its way.

The beavers were flown here to prevent that.

The beavers will build a dam.

A *dam* is a wall that holds back water and keeps it from running away.

Beavers build good dams. With their powerful teeth, they cut down thick trees. They cut the trees into logs and place them across a stream from bank to bank.

They fill the cracks and spaces between the logs with mud and sticks, until the water can no longer rush past. The beaver dam will stop the floodwater before it can rush down the mountainside. This is why forest rangers sometimes catch beavers and fly them to rivers and streams where dams are needed.

People build dams, too. In
fact, dams are among the biggest
things that people build. Many
are bigger than the pyramids of
Egypt or the biggest buildings.
Throughout the world, giant
dams hold back rivers that could
destroy thousands of farms and
homes and the lives of people
and animals. These enormous
dams let only enough water past
so that the rivers beyond can
carry it safely without overflow-
ing their banks.

But dams do more than just
hold back water to prevent
floods. Dams store water until it
is needed. Dams hold this water
in gigantic man-made lakes
called *reservoirs*.

Each year it rains and hails
and snows. But the same amount
of water doesn't fall everywhere.
Some places get so much water
that you can splash around in it.
Other places get almost none.

But when they need it, people
in many dry places can get
water that comes through pipes
from a dam's reservoir—water

for drinking and bathing, for sprinkling lawns, for use in factories, and for irrigating farms to make the food crops grow.

Long ago, Indians liked to live along riverbanks where they could catch plenty of fish to eat. But when the settlers built the first dams, the fish could no longer travel in the river to where

17

the Indians lived.

When the Indians couldn't catch enough fish, they went hungry. Many had to leave their homes because the dams had ruined their fishing.

Today whole towns sometimes have to be moved because a large dam is going to be built nearby. If the town weren't moved, it would soon be at the bottom of the dam's deep reservoir. But after the dam has been built and the water spreads out to make a lake, people have good places for camping and boating and fishing. Water fowl and wild animals often seek shelter and safety in or near the new lake.

The largest dams do something else, too. Besides holding back the water and storing it for people to use, dams also make it possible to use rushing, tumbling, falling water to make electricity. Some of the water is let out of the reservoir, or lake, through tunnels that go through the dam. Inside these tunnels are large, very special wheels called *turbines*. The water makes the wheels turn, and the turning wheels make electricity.

The electricity made by the water's pouring over the dam is carried by wires to distant places, where it works the machinery in factories that make many of the things we use every day. It also lights our cities and our homes. It cooks our meals, washes our clothes, and makes our television sets work.

Dams are so important that without them there would not be enough water in the right places to meet the needs of the many people in the world today.

You may learn more by looking up
Beavers *in Volume 2*
and Electricity *in Volume 5*.

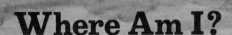

Where Am I?

The father in this picture is reading a book to his son as they float on top of the water!

How do they stay up? They aren't kicking their legs or splashing their arms to keep from sinking. There isn't a rubber mattress to hold them up. No rubber tube. No water wings. Then what *is* holding them up?

It's the salt in the water that keeps them afloat. Not just a teaspoon of salt. Not even a bucket of salt. This water is saltier than the ocean.

There's more salt in this water than in the water of any other lake in the world. If you took a glassful of this water and put it in the sun, the water would evaporate, leaving a lot of salt in the bottom of the glass.

Things float much better when water is salty. And when there is a lot of salt in the water, you just can't sink. You do have to be careful about splashing because salty water stings and hurts your eyes.

This lake, called the Dead Sea, lies between the countries of Israel and Jordan in Asia. Around the Dead Sea the air feels thick and hot and damp. No plants or animals can live there because it's too salty!

There are other salt lakes in the world. Great Salt Lake in the United States is one. It would be pretty hard for you to sink in that lake, too. But the water isn't too salty for certain shrimp and some tiny plants to live there.

Look under Where Am I? *in Volume 16*
and find the Dead Sea on the map.

America's Birthday

We all know about celebrating birthdays. But did you know that on the day you were born, a special paper was prepared just for you? It tells your name, the day, the month, and the year. It's called your *birth certificate*.

Countries celebrate birthdays too. They also have a kind of birth certificate. In the United States it is called the Declaration of Independence. It tells the day, the month, and the year that the United States declared its freedom—independence—from England and became a new country.

It happened on July 4, 1776. For days, men on horseback raced through the towns spreading the news. Bells rang. People cheered and shouted. There were parades and fireworks. Americans still celebrate their country's birthday in much the same way. Some celebrations have been extra special, like when the United States celebrated its 100th birthday in 1876. A 100th birthday is called a *centennial*. In 1976 the country celebrated its 200th birthday—its *bicentennial*—with a yearlong program of activities.

Before independence, King George of England had ruled the colonies. But the American settlers wanted to make their own rules. A long war began and was finally won—by the settlers!

During this war, the birth certificate for America was written. The men whose ideas went into this declaration came from all the colonies—now called *states*. They wrote down what they didn't like about the king's rules. They wrote about the freedoms they would like to have and how the people would fight to get them.

Most of the men who were planning the birth of America signed its birth certificate—the Declaration of Independence. Two of them—Thomas Jefferson and John Adams—became presidents of the United States. One man—John Hancock—signed his name in such large letters that to this day, when someone signs his own name, it's often called a "John Hancock."

If you liked this article,
you'll like learning about History *in Volume 7.*

Your Dentist

A dentist works in mouths.

Of course, he doesn't go inside as Jonah did with the whale, nor does he put his head inside as some lion tamers do with lions.

The dentist uses his hands and his tools to work inside mouths. Sometimes he looks inside with the help of a little mirror.

The dentist knows how important healthy teeth are for chewing food, talking, singing, and whistling.

He wants us to:

brush our teeth to keep them clean,

eat the kind of food that makes teeth strong and hard,

go to the dentist regularly for checkups.

But even when you're careful, your teeth may still cause some trouble. They may get holes in them. These holes are called cavities, and cavities make your teeth hurt. Or you might fall down and break a tooth.

When the dentist finds a cavity in one of your teeth, he digs out the bad spot and fills the cavity. Sometimes he fills it with silver or gold. The rest of the time he fills it with a hard white stuff, and it's very hard to tell that the filling isn't real tooth.

Teeth are white and shiny again after a dentist cleans and polishes them.

More About Dentists

It used to be that when a person had a toothache, he didn't go to a dentist — he went to a barber. Barbers not only gave shaves and haircuts but also pulled teeth.

There have been doctors for thousands of years, but dentists have not been around for nearly that long. Until about a hundred years ago, there weren't even any schools for dentists. If someone wanted to be a dentist, he learned by just watching and helping a dentist.

The first fillings were invented about 600 years ago. They were made of soft materials, such as gum from pine trees or wax. Later, lead and iron and gold were used. But it was hard to make fillings that fit and would not come out. Pulling bad teeth and replacing them with false teeth was much easier than trying to fill the old teeth.

False teeth were made from animal teeth and human teeth and sometimes from wood. George Washington had wooden false teeth.

Finally porcelain false teeth were made but in only a few sizes and shapes. It was a long time before the manufacturers of false teeth started making many different kinds . . . and still longer before they began to make natural-looking teeth that fit a person's mouth exactly. Today most false teeth are still made of porcelain, but some are made of plastic.

About 50 years ago, better ways of making fillings were discovered. A new kind of dentistry began at about the same time — *orthodontics,* or the straightening of teeth. By improving their teeth, as well as the shapes of their faces, an *orthodontist* helps people look better and chew better — and sometimes even talk more clearly. Perhaps you know some children who wear braces on their teeth to help straighten them.

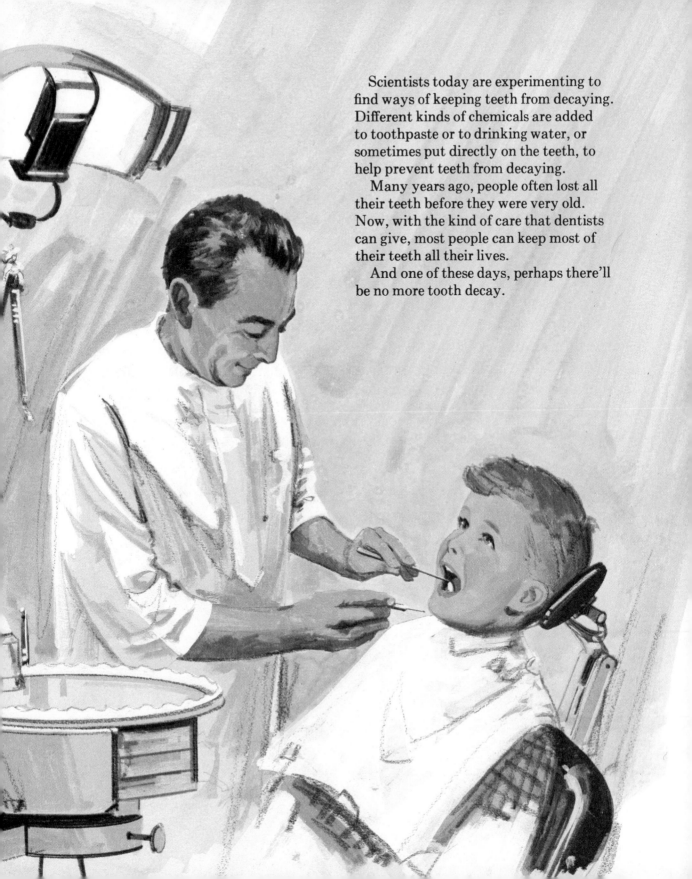

Scientists today are experimenting to find ways of keeping teeth from decaying. Different kinds of chemicals are added to toothpaste or to drinking water, or sometimes put directly on the teeth, to help prevent teeth from decaying.

Many years ago, people often lost all their teeth before they were very old. Now, with the kind of care that dentists can give, most people can keep most of their teeth all their lives.

And one of these days, perhaps there'll be no more tooth decay.

A Good Way to Cross a Desert

You could run faster than this caravan moves. A caravan is like a freight train made up of animals—often camels—instead of boxcars.

A camel "freight train" carries to market dates, spices, and other things that desert people wish to sell. And it carries back food, tobacco, tea, cloth, and things made in factories.

A camel can carry about half as much as a small truck, but you wouldn't think so if you heard it squeal when a pack is put on its back. It kneels while the pack is put on, and then it lunges to its feet and walks away through the sand as if the enormous weight were nothing at all.

Camels are good desert travelers. They don't have to drink very often. It's a good thing because there's not much water in a desert. A camel can also live for a long time on leaves and dry roots.

Caravans stop for rest during the hottest part of the day, and they stop during sandstorms.

Sandstorms may bury a camel train. The blowing, stinging sand can make the day dark. Men have to take shelter behind these big animals. After the storm the camels get up and shake off the sand.

There used to be more camel caravans moving over the deserts than there are today. Traders traveled together in a caravan to be safe from robbers. The camels were all roped together in a long line. Often a small donkey led them.

Camel trains might plod for many days and nights all the way to the seacoast. There, ship captains waited to trade things or to buy or sell. The camels got plenty of food and water to make them strong for the long trip back.

They Take Their Homes with Them

Fill 'er up!

These people, getting ready to travel across the desert to look for a new place to live, must water their camels. The camel driver tries to get each camel to drink as much water as possible because the little water that these people take along they will need themselves.

A very big camel can hold more water than some cars can hold gasoline! That's why the camel can go for many days without having to drink. It's a good thing that the camel can do this, because it may have to in the great, dry desert.

Nomads never keep their homes in one place very long. They're always moving. That's what nomads are—people who wander around instead of living in one place.

Every time the Arab nomads set out across the hot, sandy desert, it is a new adventure. They must find food for the animals, or the animals will die.

A sudden windstorm sometimes forces the nomads to stop in the middle of their search. They pull their heavy wool hoods over their faces and make the camels lie down. Then they hide behind the camels, away from the biting sand. The tougher bodies of their camels can take the blowing sand much better than their own bodies can.

Sometimes it is many days until they find grass for the animals and a water hole where they can drink. When they do, the nomads set up their tents again.

Arab nomads live in tents that can be taken down and folded quickly. The cloth for the tents is often woven from camel's hair. Some nomads still cook over a small fire built on a few rocks.

Some Arab chiefs, called *sheiks*, live in very large tents. It takes many camels to carry a sheik's belongings to a new place. If you went to dinner at a sheik's home, you would sit on pillows placed on a beautiful rug spread on the sand.

All nomads aren't Arabs, of course, and there are nomads who don't live on deserts.

In countries where there are many big cities, no one *needs* to be a nomad. Still, there are many people who like the changing life of a nomad.

Gypsies used to travel in carts—stopping now and then to trade or to buy or sell horses. They also made small things to sell, told fortunes, played music, and danced under the moon. Today many Gypsies travel in cars or trailers.

There will always be some people who like to move around and to see and live in new places. Some people live in a trailer. Whenever they want to move to a new place, they hook up their truck or automobile to their trailer and away they go. Sailors on ships might be called water nomads.

More About Deserts

A desert is a place that doesn't have enough water for gardens or farm crops to grow. Deserts can be found on every continent except Europe. Many deserts are cut off from ocean air—which brings rain—by great mountain ranges. Sometimes deserts go for years without rain. And if a little rain does fall, the air is so hot that the rain often dries up before it reaches the ground.

In the daytime a desert looks like a lost world where nothing could live. It is a hot, dry, silent place of dull grays, browns, and yellows, with heat waves shimmering over its rocks, gravel, or sand.

At night it is silvery in the moonlight and sometimes quite cold. And the desert creatures that have been hiding from the sun's burning rays come out of their lairs and burrows.

Around the water holes and springs can be heard squeaking, growling, and twittering. These sounds come from insects, pack rats, rabbits, and coyotes ... from badgers, bobcats, and foxes ... from lizards, snakes, and birds, all hunting for food and water.

Many treasures are hidden under these dry, burning deserts. Gold and silver and other minerals are there to be mined. Rich oil flows beneath the surface. But the greatest treasure of all is the underground rivers. The greatest treasure is water, which all living things must have.

Sometimes the water finds a break in the rocks and comes to the surface as a spring. When springs bubble up, plants and trees begin to grow. These islands of green are called *oases*. Without them, there could be no life in the desert. Sometimes they are very small. Sometimes they are big enough for a town to be built up around them.

With enough water, many deserts could be turned into rich farmland. California's Imperial Valley used to be one.

of the world's hottest and driest deserts. But now dams and canals bring water to it from the Colorado River, and this rich green valley grows food for thousands of people.

With irrigation and easier ways of travel, desert life is changing. In some places, airplanes and trucks are replacing camel caravans. Of all the desert animals, the camel has been the most useful. It is found in the deserts of Asia and Africa. It can go for many days without water and can carry men and heavy loads on its back.

Many people love the desert for its silence and strange beauty. In late afternoon the sky turns crimson and gold, and the mountain peaks make long purple shadows. At night the stars seem close enough to touch.

Another wonderful sight is a desert after a sudden rainfall. Then cactus plants and dead-looking bushes and trees burst into brilliant bloom.

Want to know more? Read Geography *in Volume 7 and* "How Water Gets to the City" *under* Water *in Volume 16.*

The Most Valuable Stones in the World

They sparkle and glitter in the light. No other rocks are so hard. They are very valuable. It might cost thousands and thousands of dollars to buy just one. Most are found in the ground. The largest one ever discovered is as big as a man's fist. But most are tiny.

They're diamonds!

For hundreds of years men have risked their lives searching for diamonds. To many the discovery of this glittering treasure has seemed more important than the discovery of new lands. Fairy stories tell of brave knights who battled fierce dragons and evil wizards to win kingdoms rich with diamonds.

In the Tower of London in England, there is a very special room protected by guards. There, inside a thick glass case, are jeweled crowns once worn by kings and queens. People from all over the world come to see the shimmering diamonds and other precious stones that shine from behind the glass.

Most diamonds seem to flash with a kind of white fire. But there are diamonds that sparkle in other colors, too. Sometimes diamonds are discovered in gravel at the bottom of rivers and streams. (To get these diamonds, the gravel is sucked up through giant hoses that act like vacuum cleaners.) Diamonds are found in rivers, on land, and in great stretches of hot desert sand. A few small ones are even found in or near meteorites that strike the ground from outer space.

But most diamonds are found in rocks deep inside the diamond mines of Africa. The diamonds were made millions and millions of years ago when flaming volcanoes melted a mineral called *carbon*, which was a part of these rocks. Gigantic earthquakes shook the rocks and pressed them tightly together. The hot melted carbon in the rocks was squeezed at the same time—squeezed so tightly that by the time it cooled, it had changed into the lovely hard gems called *diamonds*.

37

To get at these valuable diamond rocks, workers ride in an elevator that goes down and down into the blackness far below the ground. Tunnels connect this deep shaft with the openings—called *pipes*—inside the ancient volcanoes.

When they are first dug from the mines, diamonds don't glitter or sparkle as they do when we see them in rings or other jewelry. They look more like dull bits of glass. A man who knows all about diamonds—a diamond cutter—must cut them just right. Diamonds are so hard that nothing can cut them except the edge of another diamond.

Using his diamond-edged tools, the diamond cutter carefully removes tiny pieces so that the diamond will have many sharp edges and smooth surfaces—like little windows. It is because of these sharp edges and smooth surfaces that the diamond reflects light, sparkles and flashes with tiny bursts of color, and seems almost ablaze with fire. Diamond cutters often use diamond saws. The fine powder—diamond dust—that is left after the sawing is done can be used in a kind of sandpaper to polish the sparkling gems.

Not all diamonds are clear enough or pretty enough or large enough to be made into jewelry. But because they are so hard, they can be used for other things, such as points for drills, pen tips, and needles for record players. These diamonds are called *industrial diamonds*. Some of them are man made. Carbon is heated until it is very hot and then squeezed. If men ever learn how to make it hot enough and to squeeze it tightly enough, they will probably be able to make big diamonds. Then maybe diamonds will be cheap enough to use as buttons on your shirt or coat!

If you liked this story,
you'll like Mines *in Volume 10.*

The Man Who Believed That Children Should Have Fun

Even though Charles Dickens lived more than 100 years ago, he was your friend. He wrote stories about boys and girls and grown-ups who lived in England. Partly because of those stories, children are treated better now than they were when Dickens lived.

If she had been a real person you'd have liked Little Dorrit, who had to live in a prison house because her parents were too poor to pay the money they owed. When Dickens was young, his father and mother lived in such a place.

Charles Dickens was not much older than you when he had to quit school and take a job away from home. He worked from morning until night, with very little food to eat and only an attic in which to sleep. He tells about this in his book *David Copperfield*.

In another story Dickens tells us how children were treated in some of the schools of that time. At his own school sometimes he was beaten with the teacher's cane for laughing too loudly or for forgetting his lesson.

When Dickens tells you that Little Nell and her grandfather left home to live as beggars, you will be sad that such things could happen.

One of Dickens' best-known stories is called *A Christmas Carol*. It tells about a rich man named Scrooge, who didn't like Christmas, and about Tiny Tim, the cheerful crippled son of Bob Cratchit, a man who worked for Scrooge.

These, and many more storybook people, came from the life Dickens knew. When the stories were first read, some people were angry. Others were ashamed. Some laughed when they saw their own foolish habits acted out by people in Dickens' books. And many began to believe that children should be having fun . . . that they should not be beaten for forgetting school lessons . . . that they should not have to leave home and go to work when they are very young.

One hundred years later, people are still reading Dickens' books for the good stories that they tell.

Do you like to read about famous writers?
Look up Shakespeare *in Volume 14 or* Mark Twain *in Volume 15.*

A Life of Letters

"I do not cross my Father's ground to any House or town."

Those are the words one of America's greatest poets used when she wrote to a friend explaining that she always stayed at her family's home in Massachusetts. Emily Dickinson had many friends, but for much of her life she only wrote letters to them. When people would come to see her at her home, she often refused to see them, running upstairs to her room each time there was a knock on the door.

Emily sometimes would work on a single letter for years, writing it again and again until she finally had it just the way she wanted. She included many of her great poems in the letters she wrote. She would write or copy poems into little booklets that she made by sewing together pages with a needle and thread.

I'm nobody! Who are you?
Are you—Nobody—too?

Bee! I'm expecting you!
Was saying Yesterday

42

The poems of Emily Dickinson are thought by many people to be among the best ever written by an American. It seems strange, then, that hardly any of them were published during her lifetime. While she lived, only two were ever printed, and those without her permission.

For the time in which she lived, Emily's poems were as unusual as her own life. Unlike most of the poetry of her time, her writings did not always have exact rhymes. And even though they had few big words and were often about familiar things such as love and friendship, the poems she wrote were often hard for some people to understand. But many others saw the great beauty and truth in her thoughts and words.

Although others had been lost, Emily Dickinson left behind nearly two thousand poems for the world to read and enjoy. Despite her many friends, her greatest love was for the beauty of words. Her love for them has been felt by all who read her poems. She once wrote, "Love is like life, merely longer."

Do you like to read about famous writers?
Look up Shakespeare *in Volume 14 or* Mark Twain *in Volume 15.*

This is my letter to the World
That never wrote to Me —

I'll tell you how the Sun rose —
A Ribbon at a time —

"Hope" is the thing with feathers —
That perches in the soul —

Pterodactyl

Brontosaur

Stegosaur

Monsters of the Past

The word *dinosaur* means "terrible lizard." Although some kinds of dinosaurs were quite small, some others were the largest and scariest creatures that ever walked on land. Which one of these large dinosaurs do you think was the most terrible?

Brontosaur. The "thunder lizard" was one of the biggest of all dinosaurs, as much as 90 feet long, longer than most big houses. The frightening creature probably sounded like thunder

44

Tyrannosaur

Trachodon

Triceratops

when it walked, but it ate only plants.

Tyrannosaur. The "king of the lizards" was as long as a fire truck. It is the largest meat-eating animal ever to walk on Earth.

Trachodon. This duck-billed lizard had 2,000 teeth!

Triceratops. The "three-horned" lizard ate only plants, but it could be a fierce fighter. Many of these dinosaurs once lived in the western U.S.

45

There were many other kinds of dinosaurs, and they once lived almost everywhere. You have probably walked on the same ground that long ago was shaken by the thundering steps of these giant lizards!

Can you imagine sharing your neighborhood with dinosaurs?

Would you cross a street in front of one? Perhaps there would be a sign saying "DINOSAURS HAVE RIGHT-OF-WAY."

If you saw a dinosaur peering into your upstairs window, you'd certainly hope it ate only plants!

Speaking of food, your parents would be pretty unhappy if you invited a dinosaur home for dinner. Some of them ate more food in *one day* than you do in a whole year. Even worse, if you invited the wrong kind of dinosaur, its dinner might be you.

47

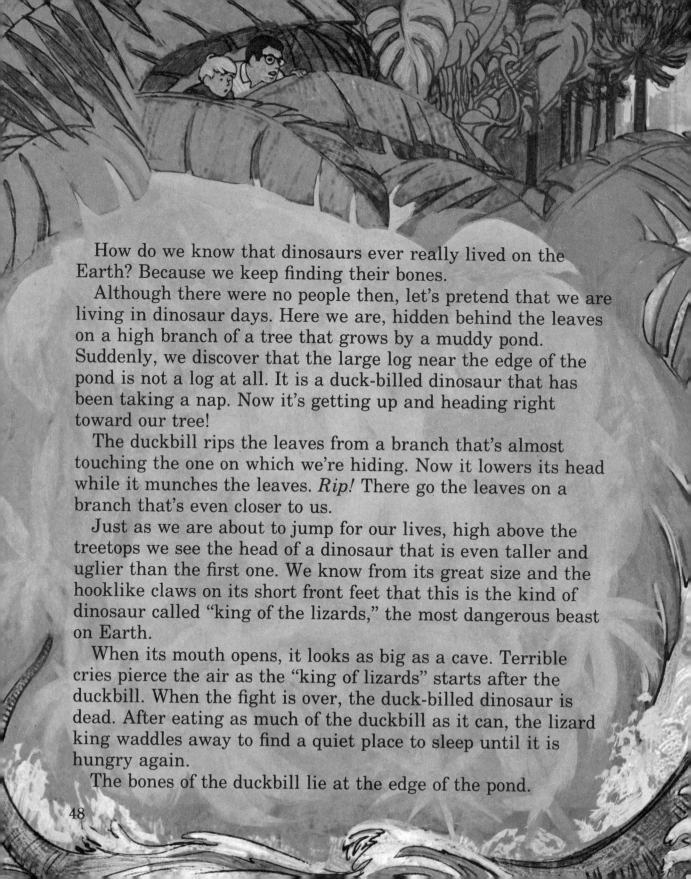

How do we know that dinosaurs ever really lived on the Earth? Because we keep finding their bones.

Although there were no people then, let's pretend that we are living in dinosaur days. Here we are, hidden behind the leaves on a high branch of a tree that grows by a muddy pond. Suddenly, we discover that the large log near the edge of the pond is not a log at all. It is a duck-billed dinosaur that has been taking a nap. Now it's getting up and heading right toward our tree!

The duckbill rips the leaves from a branch that's almost touching the one on which we're hiding. Now it lowers its head while it munches the leaves. *Rip!* There go the leaves on a branch that's even closer to us.

Just as we are about to jump for our lives, high above the treetops we see the head of a dinosaur that is even taller and uglier than the first one. We know from its great size and the hooklike claws on its short front feet that this is the kind of dinosaur called "king of the lizards," the most dangerous beast on Earth.

When its mouth opens, it looks as big as a cave. Terrible cries pierce the air as the "king of lizards" starts after the duckbill. When the fight is over, the duck-billed dinosaur is dead. After eating as much of the duckbill as it can, the lizard king waddles away to find a quiet place to sleep until it is hungry again.

The bones of the duckbill lie at the edge of the pond.

48

It begins to rain, and the rain washes the bones over the edge of the pond into the water.

More rains come and wash dirt from the bank of the pond. The dirt settles as mud over the bones. This happens for millions of years.

Slowly, as millions of more years go by, the weather changes. There is little or no rain. The sun is bright and hot. The grass and trees have dried up and blown away in hot winds. The mud that surrounded the duckbill bones is dry now, too, and nearly as hard as rock. The pond has completely disappeared. The duckbill is buried under a desert.

Who knows? Maybe nobody will ever find its bones. But maybe they will. Someday a scientist (maybe you!) might come along, looking for dinosaur bones. The scientist might dig in just the right place and find them. What a wonderful discovery!

It has happened many times before. And today in the museums of big cities, you can see these bones put together as they were when they were part of real dinosaurs millions of years ago.

Are you interested in dinosaurs?
Read Brontosaur *in Volume 2*
or Tyrannosaur *in Volume 15.*

Courtesy Field Museum of Natural History, Chicago

More About Dinosaurs

Some of the dinosaurs that once ruled the Earth were so big and strong that they didn't need to be afraid of any other living thing. How, then, did the mighty dinosaurs disappear? Why aren't there dinosaurs today?

No one knows for sure.

But we do know that at the time the dinosaurs were living, the weather began to change. The summers began to grow shorter. The winters began to grow colder. Rivers dried up, and the swamps turned into hard clay. Volcanoes erupted, throwing hot lava across the earth, and the low land pushed . . . and shoved . . . and folded back to form mountains.

With the coming of glaciers, much of the plant food that some of the dinosaurs had eaten for millions of years disappeared. The dinosaurs' bodies were so enormous that they always had to eat a large amount of food. But there were no longer any plants for them to eat.

When these dinosaurs grew hungry and thin, the dinosaurs who fed on them, in turn, could no longer find enough to eat. So they, too, grew hungry and thin.

The dinosaurs might have been too weak or too large or too stupid to move somewhere else in search of food.

Many of the dinosaur eggs were eaten by other animals.

Perhaps a disease swept across the land, killing thousands and thousands of dinosaurs. No one knows for sure.

But we do know that when the giant creatures began to disappear, other animals appeared.

These animals were smaller and more active than most of the dinosaurs. They could scurry around and find enough food to eat. Today only the bones of some of the dinosaurs are left.

52

DIRECTIONS

Flying Miles and Miles

To keep from getting lost when flying his plane from one city to another, a pilot uses many dials and clocks and lights and signals.

This monarch butterfly has no dials or clocks or lights or signals to help it. Yet butterflies like this one sometimes fly from one country, across another country, to a third country—more than a thousand miles—without getting lost.

54

In the summer, monarch butterflies are almost everywhere. You can see them in fields and city parks. Then suddenly you don't see them anymore—if you live where it's cold during the winter. They fly away south—just as many birds do—before snow falls and cold winds blow.

Butterflies aren't the only creatures that make these mysterious trips. Wild ducks and geese and many other birds make long trips every year. Why do they all do it? How do they find their way? Why do they return? From the lands around the North Pole a little bird called the *golden plover* flies southward almost all the way down to the South Pole and back again. Why? Scientists are still looking for answers to these questions.

Their first problem is figuring out where these creatures go. Although they can't follow these animals, scientists have worked out a plan to find out where they go.

Scientists and their helpers attach tags or bands to birds and other animals—even tiny butterflies—and then turn them loose.

Did you ever find a bird or a butterfly or a fish that had been marked in this way? If you ever do, write a letter to the address printed on the tag (or ask your parents to write one) and tell where and when you found the animal.

In this way we'll all learn more about where these creatures go. And someday you may be the one who discovers new things about their flights.

Another animal that seems to know where it's going is the Salmon.
Read about it in Volume 14.

Look for the Landmarks

Suppose you had never been to Cindy's house.
Suppose you asked her how to get there.
She might say, "Go straight until you come to a gas station.
Turn right. Just past a building with a flagpole on top, turn left.
When you come to a schoolhouse, you'll know you're close. Cross
the street at the corner where there's a mailbox. You'll see a white
house, then a gray house with a big pine tree in front——"

All these places that you pass on the way to Cindy's house can be used as landmarks.

Landmark sounds as if it might be a mark on the land. It could be just that—a mark that you make with a rock or a paintbrush or a piece of colored string or anything. It can be anything that is so different from the other things around it that you can see it easily and remember it. When you are trying to find your way to a place new to you and you come to a landmark that someone has told you about, you know you are going in the right direction.

Explorers in the wild places of the Earth use landmarks, too.
An explorer's landmarks may be
  a tree all twisted by the wind,
  twin hills that look like the two humps of a camel,
  a cliff that looks like a castle.
When explorers see the landmarks they are looking for, they
know they are on the right track.

Sometimes explorers go through forests or deserts or snowy
areas—places where there are no good landmarks.

What do explorers do then?

They make their own landmarks.

They may do so by bending or half breaking a small branch of a tree or by using a knife or an ax to cut away a piece of bark on a tree. This is called *blazing a trail*. Other people can follow these signs, or landmarks, to get to the places where the explorers have been.

If there aren't any trees, explorers sometimes pile rocks on top of one another to make a trail marker, or landmark.

Explorers on the ocean look for a different kind of landmark. They look for islands or rocks or lighthouses or special kinds of cliffs along the shore.

But what happens when they are out of sight of land? They can't chop a mark in the ocean or float a pile of rocks on the water to mark a trail.

No, they find their way by looking at the sun or moon or stars. For example, they know that the sun always "comes up" in the east and "goes down" in the west.

But what happens when fog or storm clouds hide the sky?

When they have no landmarks at all, explorers can find their way by using a *compass*. Maybe you have seen a compass in an automobile or a boat or an airplane. Some compasses are no bigger than a watch and even look a little like a watch. They have a "hand" that looks like the hand of a watch. It always points to the north, and from that you can figure out any of the other directions.

What are some of the landmarks to look for on the way to the place where you live?

If you liked this story,
look under Exploring *in Volume 5.*

Up High, Looking Down

You know how things look from *where you are.*

Did you ever wonder how the same things might look from *higher up?*

The lifeguard is higher up. He sits on a special platform and can see over people's heads. He can see almost everything that happens near him on the beach and in the water. His platform is near the water because he must be able to swim out quickly to save anyone in trouble.

Sometimes helicopters fly back and forth over crowded beaches looking for boats and swimmers in need of help. The helicopter crew can see much farther than the lifeguard can see. From this height swimmers seem as small as dolls, and boats look like bathtub toys. From above, you see *more,* but things on the ground look *smaller.*

Passengers in a jet plane flying overhead can look down and see the beach and also most of the city. But the passengers are up so high that the people on the beach look like specks. Skyscrapers in the city below look like ribbons on the ground.

Astronauts go so high that they can see entire countries and oceans—or sometimes the whole Earth—in one glance. From up there, mountains look like bumps, lakes and seas are patches of blue, and rivers look like winding threads. The higher they go, the more of the world they can see.

If you liked this story, you'll like Airplanes *and* Astronauts *in Volume 1 and* Helicopters *in Volume 7.*

69

The Bridge from the Ship to the Shore

Jeff stood at the rail of the great ocean liner and looked far down to where the water lapped its sides. He tried to remember how he had ever gotten onto the ship. It had been at night, long after his bedtime. He had been so sleepy that all he remembered were a lot of people everywhere and the ship's blaring whistle. Jeff knew that the sides of the ship kept going on down, far below the water. He also remembered that the time he had gone to the seashore the water along the beach was so shallow that he could wade in it. "With this boat so big," Jeff said to his father, "and sticking down so far in the water, how can it get close enough to the land so that we can get off?"

When the ship arrived at the port, Jeff found out. He clung to the rail, so excited that he could hardly stand still. Far below, two chunky little tugboats pulled the ship toward a long, two-storied concrete building that stuck out into the water.

"That's the dock," Jeff's father said. "It's also called a *pier* or a *wharf*."

Sailors on the ship threw the ends of ropes to men on the dock. The men wrapped the ropes around big posts to hold the ship. The ship's whistle made a loud "home again" sound—so loud that Jeff had to put his hands over his ears.

A kind of stairway from the ship to the dock was swung into place. Jeff's father told him that this was a *gangplank*. In a few minutes Jeff and his parents were hurrying across the gangplank to be hugged and kissed by his grandparents.

As they were all walking down the long dock, his father said, "You see, Jeff, we didn't even get our feet wet."

Jeff nodded and laughed. "It's like a bridge, isn't it? A dock is like a bridge between the land and ships on the water."

Are you interested in life on the water?
Look up Ships *in Volume 14.*

What the Doctor Can Do

It must be hard for the doctor to smile.
The only time he sees you is when you're hurt or sick—
    when your nose is stuffed up,
    when you're hot and feverish,
    when your skin is itchy,
    when something like your leg is broken,
    or when your finger is cut.
Most of the other people the doctor sees every day—sometimes
even in the middle of the night—are sick, too.

But the doctor can help because he knows how to make you well again—

to unstuff your nose

to make it not hurt so much

to make your fever go away

to make your skin stop itching

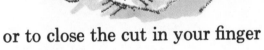

or to close the cut in your finger

to fix the broken bone in your leg

The doctor knows that even his pleasant manner makes you feel a *little* better.

Sometimes when you visit the doctor, it's just for a checkup. You're not sick. You feel fine. The doctor just wants to *keep* you feeling fine.

He listens to what's happening inside you. With his special tool called a *stethoscope,* he can hear your heart beating and your lungs breathing. He knows how they should sound when you're well.

He taps your knee with his funny rubber hammer. He watches to see how much your leg jumps. He knows just how much your leg should jump when you're well.

With his special mirror, the doctor can shine light into dark places. He looks through the hole in the middle of the mirror to see what's happening way down in your throat or in your nose or in your ears.

If the checkup shows anything wrong, the doctor often can give you medicine that will make you well before you even know you're sick.

What happens to a doctor when he gets sick? Then a doctor goes to a doctor!

If you're interested in doctors, you'll want to read Medicine *in Volume 10. To learn about the person the doctor takes care of, look under* You *in Volume 16.*

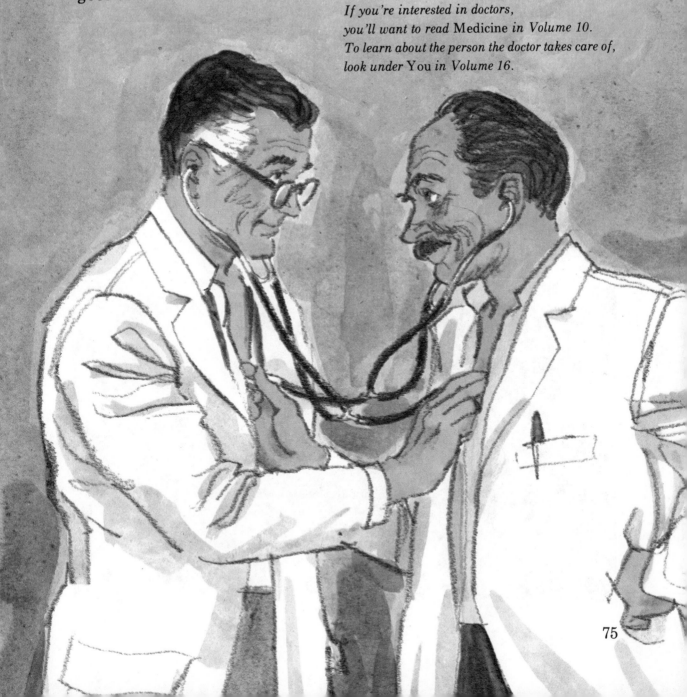

More About Doctors

Today there are all kinds of doctors— *pediatricians* (who take care of children), foot doctors, ear-nose-and-throat doctors, eye doctors, skin doctors, doctors who help with the birth of babies, doctors who set broken bones, *surgeons* (who operate on people), and many others.

But not too long ago most doctors were family doctors, who did all the things that the special doctors do now. These doctors were very important in the towns where they lived. They not only treated sick people but also set broken bones and stitched up cuts.

There were not so many hospitals then.

When a baby was born, the doctor usually went to the home. And sometimes doctors even operated on people at their homes—on the kitchen table and by the light of an oil lamp.

Until automobiles were common, these doctors made their house calls in small, horse-drawn carriages. Because these were called *buggies,* the doctors became known as horse-and-buggy doctors.

Horse-and-buggy doctors worked very hard. Often they had to get up in the middle of the night and go out in rain or snow to take care of sick people. And they didn't make much money.

Along with all the special doctors today, there are still some family doctors. They don't travel by horse-and-buggy, though. And most of them no longer go to people's homes. But they still work very hard, and they still often have to get up in the middle of the night when people are sick.

It takes a long time to become a doctor, and it takes lots of hard work. Usually a doctor is about 30 years old before he has finished all his training.

After high school a doctor goes to college. He takes lots of science courses. Then, if he has studied hard and has good marks, he can go to medical school.

In medical school he learns about the human body and about diseases. He learns how to examine people, what questions to ask them, and how to figure out what is wrong with them. Often he finds that nothing is wrong. He learns about all the special kinds of doctoring. Finally he graduates and puts the letters *M.D.* after his name, showing that he is a medical doctor.

Now he spends a year as an *intern*. An intern is a new doctor who is learning how to be a better doctor by working in a hospital. He lives in the hospital and is on call much of the time. When there is an accident somewhere, he often rides in the ambulance. The siren wails, and the cars and trucks get out of the way to let the ambulance through. At the place where the accident happened, the intern takes care of the people who are hurt. Then the ambulance takes them to the hospital.

When he finishes his internship, he may open his own office away from the hospital. But if he wants to be an eye doctor or any other special doctor, he must work in the hospital for several more years.

Even when he has finished medical school and his training in the hospital, a doctor must read and study a lot because science keeps discovering new and better ways of helping sick people get well.

DOGS

What Kind of a Dog Is That?

Andy sat on the front steps of his apartment building watching a parade of dog owners with their dogs. The dogs were being led to the playground where the big summer dog show was about to begin. Ribbons and prizes were going to be given for the best dogs.

One dog came by leading a boy! It was a l-o-n-g dog, sleek and shiny as a seal. Its short stubby legs were just high enough to keep its little round stomach from touching the ground.

"Hi, Andy," the boy called. "Aren't you going to enter *your* dog in the show?"

"I'd like to," Andy said, "but I can't decide what kind of dog he is. Unless he's a certain kind of dog, he can't enter the show."

78

"Has he got short legs like Freddy?" The boy pulled back on the leash, and Freddy stopped. "Freddy's a dachshund," the boy said. "A long time ago dogs like Freddy were used to catch badgers. Dachshunds can catch badgers right in their burrows. Their legs are so short, they can wriggle almost as well as a snake."

"My dog's legs are just about as short as Freddy's," said Andy.

"Well then, I'll bet he's a dachshund."

The boy with the dachshund moved away toward the playground, and Andy jumped up to go get his own dog and enter him as a dachshund in the dog show.

But then a boy came along trying to lead a lanky dog that was zig-zagging all over the sidewalk. First the dog would sniff at the curb. Then he would sniff at the side of a building. His hair was deep red—exactly the color of Andy's dog.

"What kind of a dog is that?" Andy asked the boy.

"Irish setter. His name is Mike. We usually keep him in the country. He's a hunting dog. He's used to running through fields of tall grass."

"My dog is the very same color as yours," said Andy.

"Oh, so you've got a setter, too! Are you going to enter him in the dog show?"

Before Andy could answer, the boy ran away holding tight to the leash that Mike was pulling.

Should he enter him as a dachshund or as an Irish setter? While Andy was trying to make up his mind, a tall girl with still a different kind of dog came along. Her dog was shaggy, with a long thin face that seemed to be mostly nose.

"What kind of a dog is that?" Andy asked.

"He's a collie," the girl replied. "His name is Brian. There are lots of collies in Scotland, because they have so many sheep there. Collies are sheep

dogs. They watch so that the sheep won't stray and get lost."

"My dog has that same kind of pointy face and those same big gentle eyes," said Andy.

"Oh, then you have a collie, too! Aren't we lucky?" The girl waved a friendly good-bye.

Right after the collie came a big short-furred dog. He was marching in front of his owner as straight as a soldier on parade. Andy's dog marched that way, too, sometimes.

"What kind of a dog is that?" Andy asked the owner, who was a boy not much taller than his dog.

"Halt!" the boy commanded the dog. The dog stopped immediately. "Sit!" The dog sat, and the boy turned to Andy. "Jet is a German shepherd. We call him Jet because he learns so fast and obeys so fast. German shepherds are used as Seeing Eye dogs. They can lead blind people safely, even through big city traffic."

"My dog is like Jet. He learns and obeys very fast!"

"Oh, so you've got a German shepherd, too." At the boy's command, Jet stood up and continued his parade march.

Dachshund, Irish setter, collie, German shepherd—Andy counted out the kinds of dogs. One more and he'd have a whole handful of dogs that were kind of like his dog!

"Hello, Andy," called Andy's teacher, a pretty young woman who was leading a tiny curly-haired dog. "Aren't you going to the dog show?"

"I'm not sure," said Andy. "Are you going?"

"No, the dog show is for you youngsters. This just happens to be the time for Pierre's walk."

"What kind of a dog is that?" asked Andy.

"Pierre is a French poodle," said his teacher.

"My dog has hair that's short and curly just like Pierre's."

"Then perhaps you've got a poodle, too."

82

Andy's teacher smiled. "They're wonderful house dogs. Such good company."

"Mine's not really a French poodle," Andy said sadly. "His hair is just curly like a poodle's. But it's the color of an Irish setter's. And his legs are short like a dachshund's. And his face is as long as a collie's. And he's as smart as a German shepherd."

"He sounds like a wonderful dog."

"Oh yes, he is," said Andy. "But I can't enter him in the dog show, because I don't know just exactly what kind he is."

Andy's teacher was staring hard at a spot just above Andy's head. Suddenly she said, "Andy, say this word after me—*dach-set-col-shep-poo.*"

"Dach-set-col-shep-poo. Dach-set-col-shep-poo!" Andy beamed. "Why, that's the kind of a dog I've got!"

"That's right. Now you hurry on over to the playground and enter him. I just know he'll win a prize!"

"Thanks, thanks a lot!" Andy jumped up and
ran to get his dog.

"What kind of a dog is that?" asked the man who was filling
out the entry blanks for the dog show.

"He's a dach-set-col-shep-poo," answered Andy.

"I've never heard of that kind of dog," said the man.

"You don't see many of them," said Andy.

"I've never seen *any* before."

"Does that mean I can't enter my dog in the show? I thought

ALL KINDS OF DOGS WELCOME

all kinds of dogs were welcome." Andy tried to keep the disappointment out of his voice.

"You're sure he's a dach-set-whatchamacallit?"

"Oh yes," said Andy, "and I can prove it!"

The man frowned. Then he got up and walked over to some people who were holding bright colored ribbons in their hands. He came back to Andy and said, "I just talked to the judges about entering your dog. It's okay."

Andy's dog won a blue ribbon for looking like more kinds of dogs than any other dog in the show.

And what was even better — the judges decided to give a special prize every year to the dog that looked like the most kinds of dogs. In honor of Andy's dog, it's called "The Dach-Set-Col-Shep-Poo Prize."

Now turn the page. Look at the dogs. What kind of dog would you like to have?

Boxer

Saint Bernard

Alaskan Malamute

Bulldog

Wirehaired Fox Terrier

Chihuahua

Pekingese

*Do you like
the animal world?
Read about* Animals
in Volume 1.

86

Great Dane

Greyhound

Bloodhound

Beagle

Boston Terrier

Cocker Spaniel

Dalmatian

87

A Dream of Dolls

Until I had the dream, I had never really thought about how many dolls there are.

Suppose that you could choose your favorites of all the dolls from every country and any time. That's what I dreamed I could do—after looking at a big picture book of dolls one night just before bedtime. It was fun! Here are the ones I chose.

A Greek child who lived more than 2,000 years ago once played with this soldier doll. I chose it because it looked just the way a warrior should look—strong and brave.

This Roman lady doll is almost as old as the Greek soldier and still beautiful.

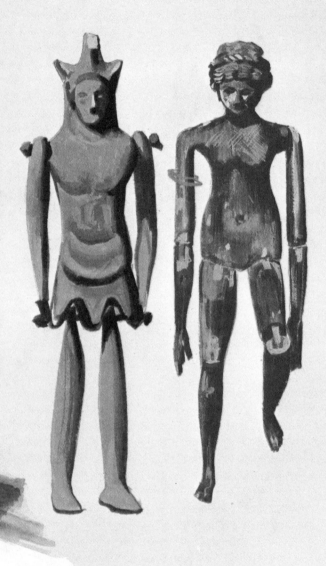

This is the way the emperor and empress of Japan looked a few hundred years ago. They are sitting on deep cushions instead of hard thrones the way some kings and queens did. The emperor and empress are wearing the fanciest clothes I've ever seen.

Some people called *Quakers* brought this doll to the United States a long time ago. I liked her because she stands so straight and tall and looks as if nothing at all would ever bother her.

This doll is carved from wood —clothes and all. She was made in England 300 years ago. I chose her because she looked so sad. I hoped that I could make her smile.

Here are eight-dolls-in-one.
Each one fits into another.
They'd be very nice in case you
had to save space on your toy
shelf.

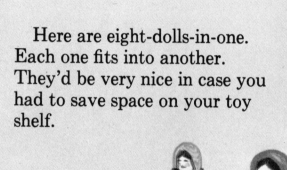

I don't think I have to explain
to you why I chose this acrobat
doll in his beaded and spangled
gold satin suit. Wouldn't you
choose him, too?

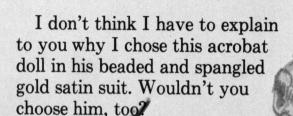

It was hard to choose toy
soldiers from the millions that I
saw. But I finally decided on
these two knights in armor.

And, of course, I chose a bride doll. She was dressed all in white just like a real bride. Why, she even had a veil and a bouquet.

I had just picked another doll off the shelf (it was about ten miles long in my dream) but *ku-lunk!* I dropped it! The sound woke me up.

When I looked around to see where the noise came from, I saw that my own very favorite doll, Suzie, had fallen out of bed.

Do you think that Suzie fell out of bed by accident? Or did she do it on purpose—to wake me up because she was jealous of my dream of dolls?

How to Build a Dream House for Your Dolls

This dollhouse was made from four boxes. With help from your mother, father, or an older brother or sister, you can make one like it. The boxes came from a grocery store. They once held such things as jars of jam and pickles and peanut butter and cans of soup. Now they have become a home to a family of dolls.

If you would like to give your dolls a home of their own, this is what you do:

Select four boxes. They may be of equal size. Or two may be large and two small.

But they should fit together so that the outer walls form a smooth line.

Someone should cut off the tops of the boxes for you.

Stack two boxes on top of the other two, open side facing out.

Cut a doorway through the walls from one room to the next—on each level. Make it high enough so that the dolls will not bump their heads as they go through.

You'll need a sharp knife—and a grown-up's help—to cut the doors.

Add as many windows as you like.

This is a good time to paint the walls with poster paint or, using glue, to paper them with gift-wrap paper.

You can make curtains from scraps of leftover cloth.

Or *paint* curtains on the walls.

The furniture and stove and refrigerator and washing machine in a dollhouse kitchen can be molded from clay.

A comfy-looking couch and deep over-stuffed chairs can also be molded from clay and then covered with pasted-on scraps of cloth.

Paste a circle of cardboard on a large spool for your dining-room table.

Smaller spools make matching chairs for the table. Cover the seats with scraps of cloth or colored paper.

Three small matchboxes stacked on top of one another make fine dressers because they have drawers that really work!

Glue them together and paint them your favorite color. Put knobs of clay on the drawers for handles.

Cut a piece of bright metal foil into squares or circles to make mirrors. You can tape or glue your mirrors on the wall above the dressers.

Beds can be made from pieces of foam-rubber sponge and cutout cardboard. The legs and bars of a baby's bed and playpen can be made of toothpicks.

Pleated paper candy cups and cookie cups turned upside down make fine lampshades.

Dabs of clay no bigger than your thumb-nail will attach the cups firmly to soda straws —thick ones, thin ones, tall or short.

Balance each straw with a bigger dab of clay at the other end of the straw.

Of course, you'll want some pretty pictures on the walls.

First, cut a sheet of heavy white paper into neat squares.

Now, with a felt-tipped pen, draw a frame around the edges of each square.

You can paint pictures of real things, such as a man, a tree, or a mountain.

Or you can make designs with bright colors.

After the pictures have dried, paste or glue them to the walls of the rooms.

And then put out the welcome mat!

They Swim Like Fish

Splish! Splash!
A whistle blows, and slick, shining gray creatures swim around and around in the big tank. Faster and faster. And then . . .

They leap out of the water. Up, up, up into the sunlit air. For a moment the great gray creatures are like birds flying. One after the other they leap up to snatch fish from the hand of their trainer, who is standing on a high platform.

The show is on! And it's one of the most amazing animal shows you could ever see.

Dolphins live in water and swim with fins. They look like fish. They swim like fish.

But they aren't fish. They're whales. Small whales. (You can see how a *big* whale looks swimming next to a dolphin!)

Dolphins need to stick their heads out of water to breathe. Otherwise they would drown. They even have a special hole on top of their heads for blowing air in and out.

The dolphin you see at the bottom of this page has a funny name—bottle-nosed dolphin. That's because its nose is shaped like the neck of a bottle.

And now . . . on with the show.

97

The trainer tosses rubber rings out over the water in the tank. The dolphins seem to dance back and forth on their tails as they jump through the whirling hoops.

Then there might be a basketball game, with the dolphins bumping balls into a basket with their rubbery heads. The show ends when they catch silly hats to wear over their beaklike noses.

The friendly, playful dolphins look as if they're having as much fun as the people watching them.

You might think that dolphins are most at home in water tanks. But their real home is in the ocean.

It would be strange to see a dolphin swimming by itself. Dolphins travel together—sliding down the waves made by ships (like a toboggan ride) or rolling on their sides in the foam.

There are many stories of dolphins using their heads to bump swimmers in trouble to the shore. And if they see an injured dolphin under the water, they sometimes nudge it to the top so that it can get air to breathe.

There is only one creature that the dolphin has been known to attack—the shark. And that is just about the fiercest fish of all. A group of angry dolphins will ram their heads at a shark until the shark is killed or swims away.

One of the many amazing things a dolphin can do is to make "talking" sounds. They make more different sounds than any other animals except people.

Dolphins whistle, bark, squawk, squeak, and make clicking sounds. Many people who have studied dolphins believe that each sound means something different. Dolphins use a certain kind of whistle when they are frightened. They make other sounds when they are hungry or angry or just playful.

Some scientists think that dolphins are "talking" to each other in their own special way when they make these sounds. No one knows for sure. But we do know that dolphins can learn all kinds of difficult tricks. They are very, very intelligent— perhaps among the most intelligent creatures on Earth.

Someday, someone might prove that dolphins are having real conversations. Just like people—only with dolphin sounds.

You may read about Whales *in Volume 16. If you're interested in underwater life, read* Aquanauts *in Volume 1.*

More About Dolphins

Miss Margaret Howe's special living room was full of water. The water was not very deep—only up to her knees. She lived in this watery room with two friends named Peter and Pam. Miss Howe walked around in the water, but her two friends had to swim.

Peter and Pam were dolphins!

Miss Howe lived in a specially built house with these dolphins. They were her students, and she tried to teach them to speak as people do.

"Hello," said Miss Howe.

"Hello," said Peter.

"Do you want to play ball?" asked Miss Howe.

"Ball," answered Peter.

Peter was actually speaking in sounds that anyone could understand. He was imitating Miss Howe. It had taken her many months to teach these dolphins to say just a few words. But she had succeeded!

Under the water and out of the water, dolphins can make many different and interesting sounds. They not only have their own sounds but also can imitate just about anything—fish, motors, and humans.

Dogs and cats make many different sounds, too, so why do we say that dolphins are talking but not dogs and cats? Also, we can teach parrots and some other birds to imitate our words, so what is so special about dolphins?

Many people think that when dolphins make some of their sounds, they are actually talking—*and that they may even know what they are saying*. No one has ever been able to prove this for sure, but Miss Howe and a man named Dr. Lilly are trying to prove it.

Dolphins have brains that are bigger than ours and almost as complicated. Miss Howe and Dr. Lilly have been studying dolphins for many years. They think that dolphins want to talk to us as much as we want to talk to them. That is why Dr. Lilly built a special laboratory, and that is why day after day Miss Howe splashed around in the water trying to teach Peter and Pam Dolphin how to speak.

When Miss Howe was living with Peter and Pam, she got up every day at 7:30 in the morning. From 8:00 to 8:30 she had her first English lessons of the day with Peter, then with Pam. Classes continued for the rest of the day, with Miss Howe teaching Peter and Pam their words and numbers.

More than anything else, though, Peter and Pam loved to play games with Miss Howe. They played catch with a ball. They played tag and many other games in the water. But Miss Howe was always ready to teach them new words. She tried to help them understand how we think and why we do many of the things that we do.

If dolphins and people *could* learn to talk to each other and to understand each other, dolphins might be able to tell us many things that we don't know about the ocean.

The Donkey's Shadow

One hot summer's day a young man hired a donkey and a driver to take him to the next town. Carrying the young man, the donkey trudged along the dusty road, while the driver walked ahead.

The afternoon sun became so hot that the young man told the driver to stop. The only shade was the donkey's shadow, and so the man settled himself there.

But the driver said, "Wait! *I* want to sit there."

"Didn't I hire the donkey for the whole trip?" asked the young man. "There isn't enough shade for both of us."

"Yes, you hired the donkey," the driver said, "but you certainly said nothing about hiring its shadow."

And as they stood in the road and argued, the donkey kicked up its heels and ran away, taking its shadow with it.

Downtown

Downtown!
Rush! Crush!
Lots of noise!
Bang! Bam!
Buses! Trucks!
What a jam!
What a busy traffic cop!
Green—*Go!* Red—*Stop!*
People stream
Through the doors
Of a thousand
Shops and stores.
To and fro
Rush the crowds.
The buildings almost
Touch the clouds.
A little boy
Tries to see
How far up
The top can be.
Is he lost?
No, they'll find him.
Mother's not
Too far behind him.
In the middle
Of the street
A pigeon looks
For things to eat.
He's the only one for whom
Downtown's just
A dining room!

Let's Go Shopping

Suppose you wanted to buy—
    a big blue hat
    or a tame white rat,
    a red clown suit
    or a bright toy flute,
    a one-wheeled bike
    or a sidewalk trike,
    or a doll as big
    as a farmer's pig.

In a big city you could probably find all these things. Downtown in a city you can buy nearly anything you can think of.

Good things to eat are brought
into the city at night from farms
and factories.

Trucks and trains and boats
and planes bring milk and meat—
and vegetables, fish, and fruit.
Airplanes carry live lobsters,
oysters, and clams from the
ocean and fresh fruits from warm
countries.

Are you hungry?

Downtown in a city you are never far away from a hot dog or a hamburger, an ice-cream cone or a candy bar. Or popcorn, peanuts, or orange juice.

You can even find unusual things like hot chestnuts and big chewy pretzels—and still stranger things to eat from lands far away across the ocean.

And downtown is where your mother and father probably go to buy big, household things like a refrigerator, a stove, or a television set.

At a book store you can get all kinds of books—books that teach things and books just for fun. And the record shop has everyone's favorite songs and music on records.

Large department stores sell all kinds of clothing and shoes for everyone from the baby to Grandpa.

The things you buy at the downtown stores come to the city from many parts of the world. The workers who made these things are paid money for making them. The workers use the money they get to buy things when *they* go shopping.

Life in the city can be very interesting.
Read about it under City *in Volume 3 or under* Night *in Volume 11.*

The Mayor's Busy Morning

"Good morning, Mr. Mayor."
Miss Collins smiled as Mayor Herzog hurried into his office. Miss Collins was the mayor's secretary.

The mayor unbuttoned his heavy blue coat and put his bulging briefcase on the desk.

"Your wife called," Miss Collins said. "You forgot to tell Henry whether he could go to the basketball game after school. And she wants to know if you'll be home for dinner."

The mayor sighed. "Sometimes I wish I were four people instead of one. Please call my wife back and say yes, Henry can go to the basketball game, and no, I probably won't be home for dinner. But first, what's on the calendar for today?"

John Herzog was mayor of a large city. His job kept him very busy. Every day brought new problems.

Like most mayors, Mr. Herzog had to find out what the people of the city wanted. And he had to find the right people to do all the jobs that keep a city going.

"Let's see," Miss Collins began. "You have a meeting with the visiting mayors' committee this morning. Then a luncheon for the boys' club. There's a parade at two o'clock. Then a meeting with newspapermen at four. Chief of Police Polland will be here to talk with you about the new squad cars before you leave for the school-board dinner."

Just then the phone rang.

"It's Mr. Singer, Your Honor," Miss Collins said.

Mr. Singer was chairman of the school board.

"John," he began, "I hope you can see me before the school-board meeting on Thursday.

We're going to have to get more money somewhere if the city is going to build three new schools."

The mayor nodded to himself. There were always money problems. Not only for schools but also for parks and garbage pickup, for streetlights and transportation, and for clean water and all the many other city services. Big cities just kept getting bigger. Sometimes there was enough money. And sometimes there wasn't.

"We'll meet tomorrow morning," Mayor Herzog said, "and we'll talk about it then."

Miss Collins wrote the new appointment on his calendar. A mayor needed someone to help him keep track of all his plans, just as he needed good people to do the work of running the city.

A buzzer sounded.

"Whoever that is, I'll have to see him later," the mayor said, putting on his coat again. "I want to see Judge Hammond before I meet with the visiting mayors' committee."

"Don't forget your briefcase, Mr. Mayor," Miss Collins called after him.

Mayor Herzog stopped, smiled, and took a deep breath. "All these problems in just one city! I wonder what it's like to be president of a whole country."

Miss Collins laughed, "I'm sure the president must forget his briefcase sometimes, too, Your Honor."

Mayor Herzog understood. "I guess each man just does the best he can," he said. And he walked down the hall, smiling and shaking hands with some schoolchildren who were waiting to see what a real mayor looked like.

Monsters That Eat Fire

R-o-a-r. . . .

It's not a lion. It's a roar a hundred times as loud as a lion makes.

W-h-o-o-s-s-h-h. . . .

That's fire and smoke coming out of its mouth!

But you don't have to be afraid. All of the fire-eating dragons are tucked between the covers of books, along with lots of other imaginary creatures. They appear in stories about

brave and handsome knights and princes who rode throughout the land on prancing horses.

The knights and princes were looking for adventure or for something magic or for a great treasure, or perhaps they wanted to save a beautiful princess.

From what do you think they wanted to save the princess?

Quite often it was a dragon—a dreadful, terrible, fierce, fire-eating, monstrous dragon!

In those long-ago storybook days, there were all kinds of dragons. But you could always recognize a dragon when you found one or when it found you! Dragons roamed the land, swishing their great scaly tails. They flashed fiery glances from their enormous eyes. They blew rings of poisonous smoke and breathed out flames of fire without ever burning their tongues!

Or at least some of the dragons did. Others, mostly dragons from China and the Far East, breathed out mist and clouds instead of smoke and fire. Some people said that these dragons, if they wanted to, could make the rain fall or stop it from falling.

Some dragons were cute little fellows no bigger than your finger. Others were bigger than the longest city street. Some lived underneath castles. Others were so huge and thirsty that they could drink a whole river dry in one long, wet gulp. But that still didn't put the fire out in their mouths.

Some dragons were both small and large. They were shape changers that were always making themselves into something new or different. They changed themselves into red dragons, two-headed dragons, and, tricky as they were, even handsome princes.

Most dragons were fierce and angry. Maybe they were so disagreeable because they never slept. Most dragons never closed all of their eyes at the same time. Often they would stare with only one eye.

A few dragons were friendly and kind. They were castle pets and sometimes guarded precious treasures for a prince or a princess or protected a sacred spring.

Others were shy and timid. They were afraid to protect anything at all.

The fiercest, meanest dragons were always up to tricks. They insisted on standing by a turn in the road, and should anyone dare to pass by, the dragons tried to gobble him up.

Some dragons wouldn't let anyone near their favorite river or lake. Others lived in mountain caves and wouldn't let anyone climb up. Quite often the dragon was guarding a treasure of gold or jewels inside the cave. Sometimes it guarded a magic *talisman*, a key that a knight or a prince had to get before he could rescue a sleeping princess.

Some dragons loved princesses . . . for dinner.

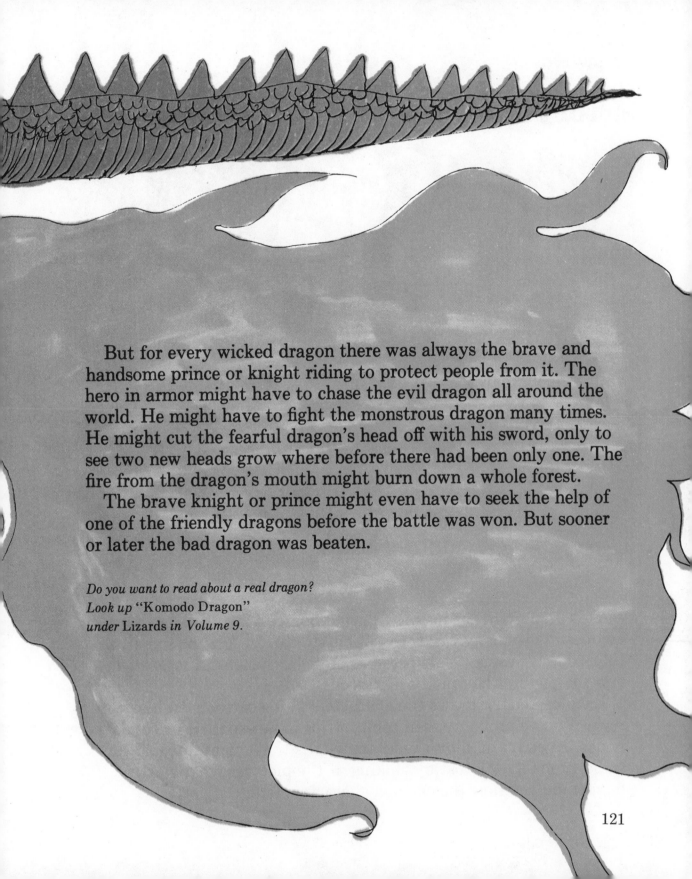

But for every wicked dragon there was always the brave and handsome prince or knight riding to protect people from it. The hero in armor might have to chase the evil dragon all around the world. He might have to fight the monstrous dragon many times. He might cut the fearful dragon's head off with his sword, only to see two new heads grow where before there had been only one. The fire from the dragon's mouth might burn down a whole forest.

The brave knight or prince might even have to seek the help of one of the friendly dragons before the battle was won. But sooner or later the bad dragon was beaten.

Do you want to read about a real dragon?
Look up "Komodo Dragon"
under Lizards *in Volume 9.*

Storyteller with a Pen

This man sitting at his big drawing board is a storyteller. But he doesn't use many words to tell his stories. In fact, he sometimes doesn't use any. He uses pictures. He is called a *cartoonist*, and the pictures he draws are *cartoons*.

Each cartoonist draws the characters in his cartoons in his own style. You've probably seen comic strips in newspapers or comic books. Even if you didn't read any words that might appear, you could probably tell just by looking at the pictures what was happening and how the cartoon characters felt.

What is the difference between these two pictures? The cartoonist has drawn everything the same way . . . except for the boy's mouth. Just by changing one curved
line, he has made a smiling boy sad.

If you look closely, you can see that by changing circles into straight lines, the
cartoonist has closed eyes that were open.

Sometimes the artist changes more than one line. If he wants the boy to run, he might do this

Or this

With the arms this way, the boy looks surprised.

This way he looks sad.

Here are some easy ways to draw

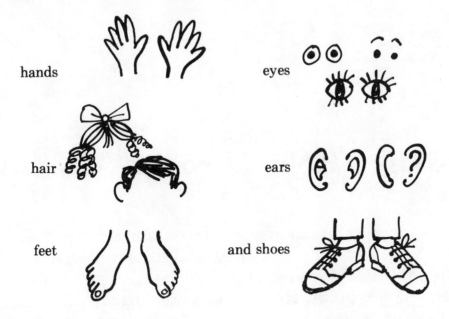

hands

eyes

hair

ears

feet

and shoes

Remember the first picture you saw? It looked like this one . . . except that now the cartoonist has added something new —a dog. If you were the artist and wanted to make the dog happy or sad or surprised, how would you draw it? Would you change its eyes? Its ears? The way it stands or sits? Here are some dog eyes and ears to use in your drawing.

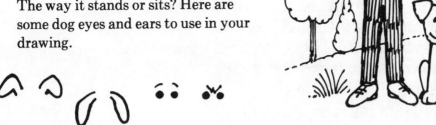

If you liked this story,
you'll like "Paint Something Different Today"
under Art *in Volume 1.*

How to Dig a Hole–Through Anything

Men and women were standing near the entrance of the coal-mine shaft. All looked sad and worried, and some women were crying. Far under the ground a tunnel had caved in and some miners were trapped inside. Rescuers had been digging all day long, but twice there were new cave-ins. The miners had no food or water, and their air would be gone soon.

But the people had a plan for helping the miners. A heavy truck was parked at a point directly above where the men were trapped. It was not an ordinary truck. From its trailer rose a great hollow mast as tall as a tree. Inside the mast was a *drill*—a machine that could make a round hole deep down into the ground.

In the truck a powerful diesel engine roared, driving the drill downward. The great arm of the drill was hammered steadily into the ground. The machinery turned after each hammer blow and hammered again and again. The drill had been working for a long time, pushing down through earth and rock. Now suddenly the men operating the drill gave a shout and shut off the motor. The drill had gone through into the mine tunnel!

The people above called down through the drill hole. They heard the men's voices, far below, answering. Now the miners would have fresh air to breathe. Food and water could be lowered to them, and they could live until the mine tunnel could be cleared so that they could come out.

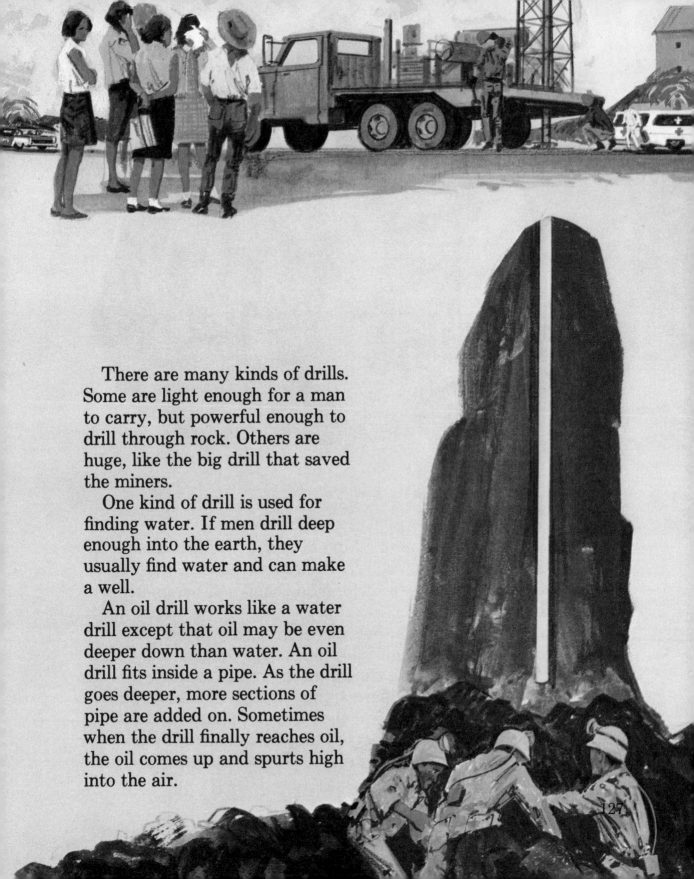

There are many kinds of drills. Some are light enough for a man to carry, but powerful enough to drill through rock. Others are huge, like the big drill that saved the miners.

One kind of drill is used for finding water. If men drill deep enough into the earth, they usually find water and can make a well.

An oil drill works like a water drill except that oil may be even deeper down than water. An oil drill fits inside a pipe. As the drill goes deeper, more sections of pipe are added on. Sometimes when the drill finally reaches oil, the oil comes up and spurts high into the air.

127

Cavemen long ago also used a kind of drill. It worked in almost the same way as the rescuer's drill. The caveman's drill was a pointed piece of rock that was held in one hand and hammered with another rock.

When men began to make tools out of iron, they could drill through solid rock. More than 2,500 years ago, Greeks on the island of Samos drilled a long tunnel through solid rock.

In Egypt, miners used a different kind of drill—one that spun very fast as it was pushed against the rock. Both kinds of drills are still used today, though now they are much more complicated. They are run by motor and can drill holes faster and deeper than the old drills could.

Sometimes holes are drilled just to find out what is in the ground. A hollow drill cuts out a piece of ground, called a *core sample,* that is brought up to the surface and studied. If these core samples are stretched out in a long row, in the same order in which they come out of the ground, they can show exactly what is down there. It might be mud, clay, sand, rock, slate, coal —or anything.

The Place for Medicine and More

When Sandy fell off her bicycle and scraped her knee, her mother put a bandage on the cut. When her mother noticed that she had used the last bandage in the box, she sent Sandy to the store to buy some more.

Mr. Mayberry went to the doctor because his stomach was upset. The doctor wrote some words on a small piece of paper and handed it to Mr. Mayberry. The paper was a *prescription* for the kind of medicine that would make him feel better. The doctor told Mr. Mayberry to take the prescription to a store to get the kind of medicine he needs.

Jerome wasn't feeling sick at all. He just wanted a magazine about video games, the kind with pictures of all the latest ones.

All three of these people went to the same store. They went to a drugstore.

Sandy found lots of different bandages on a shelf in the middle of the store. Jerome didn't need any help to find the magazine he wanted. Mr. Mayberry *did* need help to get the kind of medicine his doctor wanted him to have. Since he had a doctor's prescription, he needed to talk to the *pharmacist,* a person who works in the drugstore and has had years of training to learn about all kinds of different medicines. Pharmacists are sometimes called druggists.

It did not used to be that way. From very early times people have searched for things to take away pain or sickness. They tried leaves of plants, roots, flowers, parts of animals or insects, oils, and other things.

Some of these things worked, or seemed to work, but most of them did not. In time some people claimed to know more about

these medicines than other people. In certain places these people were called medicine men.

Mr. Mayberry handed his prescription to the pharmacist behind a counter near the back of the store. The prescription told the pharmacist what kind of medicine Mr. Mayberry should have, how much of it he should be given, and the best times for taking it.

The pharmacist didn't take much time to give Mr. Mayberry his medicine. After reading the prescription, she got a large bottle of pills and put a few of them into a small bottle. Then she typed out the name of the medicine and the times Mr. Mayberry should take each pill. She attached the paper to the bottle and gave the medicine to Mr. Mayberry.

Today, most medicines are made in big factories. The places where medicine is made are kept extremely clean so that dangerous germs and dirt will not get mixed in with the drugs that are being made. Each kind of medicine is tested again and again to be sure that it works as it should.

The pharmacist buys the medicine from the people who make it. The pharmacist has to know how to take care of the medicines. Some need to be kept in a refrigerator so they will not spoil. Others need to be kept completely dry. Many kinds of medicine become weak if they are not used quickly enough, so the pharmacist has to watch the dates on the drugs to be sure that none is too old to be useful.

Every year, new kinds of medicines are being tested and then manufactured and sold to drugstores. Pharmacists need to learn about some of these new medicines every year to be sure that they can be given safely to people just like you!

If you liked this story, you'll like Doctors *on page 72 in this book and* Medicine *in Volume 10.*

DRUMS

Listen to the Talking Drums

A long time ago when there were no telephones—and not even a mailman—how do you think people sent messages quickly?

They didn't.

There was no way they could send a quick message to friends who lived over a hill or far away. They couldn't shout loud enough for people to hear. If they were out in the woods and saw a dangerous animal running toward their village, there was no way they could warn their friends.

People in those days must have wondered, "What can we use that will make more noise than our voices? It must be something that is loud enough to be heard very far away."

134

Perhaps one day a man sat on the ground thinking about this problem. As he sat, he might have tapped a stick on a log that was hollowed out from rotting. He might have noticed the *clonk-clonk* sound that came from the log—and maybe that was where he got his idea for making a drum!

Somebody had to be the first one, and if it was this man, we can imagine that he took the partially hollowed log and hollowed it out even more with his stone knife. Then he—or someone else one day—took a piece of animal skin and stretched it over the end of the hollow log.

To hold the skin down, he might have tied a thin strip of animal hide around the log. Or he might have wrapped a vine tightly around it, or a rope that he had made by weaving grasses. With any of these he could have tightened the skin on the end of the hollow log.

His invention was finished! Now to use it. We can imagine that he hit the tightly stretched skin with his hand. It made a loud *boom!* He hit it again. *Boom—boom!* He moved his hand all around the skin to find the best place to hit it. Each place made a slightly different sound.

The drum was heard very far away. Even the men who had been hunting in the woods ran to the village to find out what was making the loud noise.

It was so long ago that we can only imagine how that first drum was made. But we do know that the drum has been important to many different people all over the world.

In some places in Africa even today, a drummer will beat a drum in the evening to tell the people in nearby villages the many things that have happened in his village during the day. He may tell of a baby being born or of an old man dying. If we heard the drums, we wouldn't know what they were saying. But to the African people who have learned the language of the drums, the drums carry information.

In Africa drums are sometimes used to warn people that a dangerous animal is near. Often they are used to call people to a meeting, as we might use a big bell.

African drums make a very loud and frightening noise when they call the men of the village to war. But they make a happy, gay sound when the people are celebrating the winning of a war or when they are having a big feast. Then the people sing and dance to the beat of the drums.

There are many different kinds of drums. Sometimes the Africans stretch an animal skin over both ends of a log. We see double-headed drums today in most of our bands and big orchestras.

Sometimes the skin is stretched over a clay pot or an iron pot. The iron pot drum is called a "kettle" drum. Our big orchestras today have drums that are called *kettledrums*.

The African people also make a tambourine. Maybe you have a toy tambourine. It is a very small drum held in one hand and played with the other. But the drum that makes the most noise of all is the big bass drum. Some are so big that two men have to carry them. You can see them in parades when people are marching. They go *bom—bom—bom—bom!*

You may learn about another way of signaling if you read "Smoke Signals" *under* Signs and Signals *in Volume 14.*

More About Drums

It may look as if these men are pounding on a bunch of old cans. But if you heard them, you'd know the difference. You'd know that they are making music on drums.

The drums *are* made from cans, though. Many people in the islands of the West Indies make their own musical instruments, especially drums. And often they make their drums out of old cans that storm waves have washed up on the ocean beach or out of empty cans from stores or factories.

Some of these drums are very big—so big that three or four children could get inside one. Before these cans were used as drums, they were full of oil. Even then they were called *drums—oil drums!*

The other drums in the "can band" are smaller. They once held crackers or tea or molasses or fish or spices or almost anything.

The sound that a drum makes when struck with drumsticks depends on its size.

Some big drums *boom*. Some smaller drums *ping*. Some make high, tinkly sounds. Others make low, rumbling noises. And when tapped in the middle, each drum sounds slightly different from what it sounds like when tapped closer to the edge.

Boys and girls in the West Indies collect all these different-sized drums. They practice by themselves first before practicing together in a drum band.

But you don't have to go to the islands of the West Indies to find drums. You can find them almost everywhere. Start looking. They're all around you. You probably just haven't noticed them.

Turn some empty tin cans and some pots and pans upside down and start tapping. Tap them with two spoons or pencils—almost any old sticks will do. You can also tap cardboard boxes. They make a different sound. The round ones that have held oatmeal or cornmeal are especially good.

Keep trying different empty containers until you find the ones that sound best to you.

Champion Swimmers

What's going on here? We can see a feathered tail and a big webbed foot.

No head! No neck!

What's going on?

It's a duck poking its long beak into the muddy bottom of a stream to find food—an insect, or perhaps a shellfish hidden down there.

Ducks are at home almost anywhere near water. Some feed and nest in streams and ponds. Others live near deep, wide lakes. Some make their homes on rocky cliffs by the ocean.

The ducks on this page don't stand on their heads to get food. They dive straight down into a lake or ocean to snap up fish and water plants. They can stay under water for a long time.

Ducks are champion swimmers. And they fly high and gracefully over mountains and tall buildings. But on the ground? With feet that seem too big for their bodies, they waddle from side to side, moving slowly in a funny, jerky way!

Even though ducks usually fly south in the wintertime, the iciest water doesn't seem too cold for them. A thick coat of feathers keeps them warm. And it's waterproof. Feathers are a duck's raincoat!

The tiniest, fluffiest duck feathers—called *down*—are used to line the nest and keep the eggs warm when the mother duck is away.

Most nests are built in hollows near the water. But many are attached to the tall stalks that grow over marshy ponds. Some ducks even look for holes in the tops of trees to make nests for their eggs.

Baby ducklings don't need to *learn* how to swim. They *know!*
The minute these soft, downy baby birds waddle out of the nest,
they head for the water.

And here's a strange thing. As soon as their babies are hatched,
the grown-up ducks start losing their feathers. Until new feathery
coats are grown, the ducks can't fly. So they hide in the grasses
along the shore to keep safe from enemies.

They fly, they waddle.
They swim with ease.
They build their nests in stalks and trees.
On land, in lakes,
Or high in the air,
Ducks live almost anywhere!

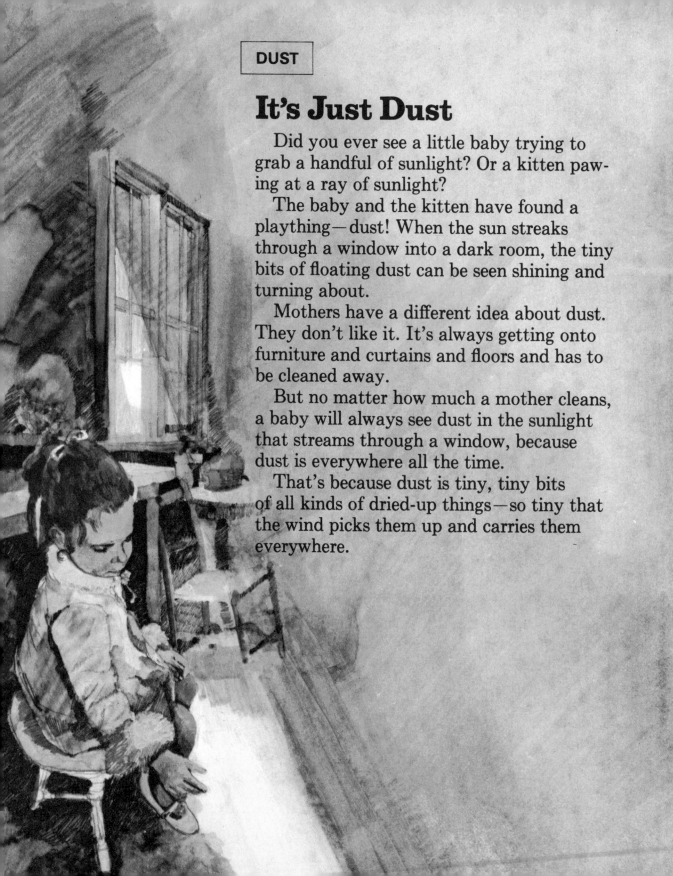

It's Just Dust

Did you ever see a little baby trying to grab a handful of sunlight? Or a kitten pawing at a ray of sunlight?

The baby and the kitten have found a plaything—dust! When the sun streaks through a window into a dark room, the tiny bits of floating dust can be seen shining and turning about.

Mothers have a different idea about dust. They don't like it. It's always getting onto furniture and curtains and floors and has to be cleaned away.

But no matter how much a mother cleans, a baby will always see dust in the sunlight that streams through a window, because dust is everywhere all the time.

That's because dust is tiny, tiny bits of all kinds of dried-up things—so tiny that the wind picks them up and carries them everywhere.

Anywhere that there is a dry yard without grass or a field without plants, the wind finds dust. As the bare earth dries, the wind sweeps up the tiny pieces and carries them away.

Once, a great many farms in the United States simply blew away. At least the *topsoil* blew away. (The topsoil is that part of the earth that growing things put their roots into.)

The farmers had let too much of their land get bare. Then the rain did not fall for a long, long time. When strong winds blew, they swept up the dry, dusty earth.

There was so much dust in the air that it was hard for people to see. The dust piled high against houses, and it buried sidewalks and fences.

This area became known as the Dust Bowl. Since then farmers have learned how to manage their farms better. They plant crops that don't dry up and leave the ground bare if it doesn't rain. They don't let cows chew the grass down to bare ground. And they plant trees in rows to stop the blowing dust.

People stir up dust in many ways. Any time that they use machines to grind, cut, or polish things, they make dust. There can be paper dust from a paper mill, flour dust from a flour mill, or coal dust from a coal mine.

If you're going to school, you know how much dust you can make just cleaning blackboard erasers.

All dust is dry. But strangely enough, rain won't fall unless there is dust in the air. For each drop of rain forms from tiny droplets of water that gather around a single speck of dust. When the droplets form into heavy drops, they fall out of the clouds.

The rain falls to the earth, wetting the dust on the ground and making mud. But the sun shines again, and the wind blows . . . then the mud dries up, and we have dust again.

Sometimes germs that cause sickness get attached to dust specks. When the dust gets into a house, the germs come right along. Of course, mothers don't like germs that can make their families sick, so they try to get rid of dust as fast as they can. And they tell you to wash your hands before you touch the food you eat.

Yet, if your mother should get *too* upset about dust, remind her of rainbows. Rainbows are beautiful—and they come with the rain. And rain—remember—has to have dust before it can fall. And besides, anything that can make babies and kittens happy can't be all bad.

The Colors We Wear

Grass and leaves grow green, and flowers grow in reds, yellows, blues, and nearly every other color. But what made your shirt red, your skirt blue, or your sweater brown? *They* didn't grow that way!

Dyes did it. Red dyes, blue dyes, green dyes, yellow dyes, purple dyes—dyes of every color! Dyes color your clothes.

What are dyes? Where do they come from?

The first time people wore colors, it wasn't in their clothes. It was on their skin! Many years ago people discovered that they could rub certain plants on their skin and make colored designs.

Some of the first people to dye their clothes were the Egyptians. They discovered that a plant called *indigo* made a very pretty blue color when it was boiled in water. If they put their clothes in the same water, the clothes would turn the same blue color.

As time passed, people began to find more and more things that made color—flowers, fruits, roots, and bark. These would make dyes of their own color when they were boiled in water. Walnut and butternut *hulls* (outside covers) made brown dyes, daffodils and sunflowers made yellow dyes, blueberries made blue purple dye, red tulips and cranberries made red dyes, and blackberries made black dye. Pioneers in early America used to have special gardens filled with plants for making dyes.

These early dyes were borrowed from plants, but men soon began to wonder whether they could make their own dyes. They studied the dye plants very carefully to find out how they made their colors. Finally men began to make their own dyes in factories.

Dyes today are so easy to use that almost anybody can dye clothes. To see how easy it is to dye clothes, let's look at how a little girl named Hannah dyed her own blouse.

Hannah and her mother had just returned from the grocery store when Hannah saw her mother take two small boxes from the grocery bag and place them on the table near the sink.

"What's in those boxes, Mother?" Hannah asked.

"In one box is red dye for my dress, and in the other is yellow dye for your old blouse," her mother answered.

"May I help dye my blouse?" Hannah asked.

"I don't see why not," her mother said. "And maybe we can try something special with your blouse."

"Something special?" Hannah's eyes widened.

"You'll see," her mother said.

Hannah watched excitedly as her mother took two very large metal pots from the kitchen cupboard. She filled them half full with water and put them on the stove to boil. Then she poured red powder from one of the boxes into one of the pots and yellow powder from the other box into the other pot. The water became colored.

After the water started to boil, Hannah dropped her blouse into the yellow dye, and her mother put her dress into the red dye.

"We'll stir these in the dyes for a while, and soon they'll be bright new colors," Hannah's mother said.

Hannah and her mother took the blouse and the dress out of the water after a few minutes. They hung them over the sink to dry.

Hannah's mother emptied the yellow dye into the sink but kept the red dye on the stove.

"Now we're going to do something special with your blouse," she said. "As soon as the blouse is dry, you can tie knots in the sleeves."

"Tie knots in the sleeves?" Hannah thought this was a strange thing to do, but she wanted to see what would happen next. When the blouse was dry, she tied two knots in each sleeve.

Into the red dye went the bright yellow blouse.

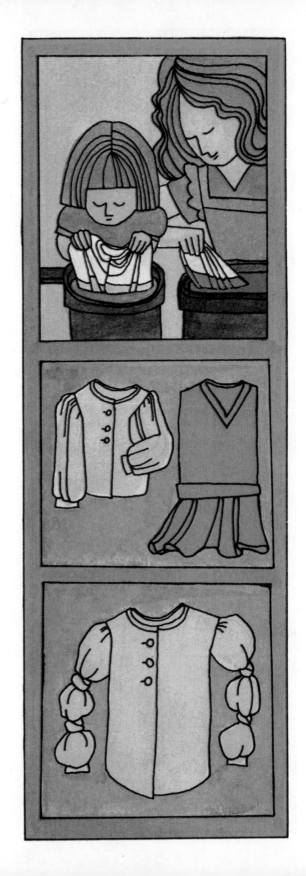

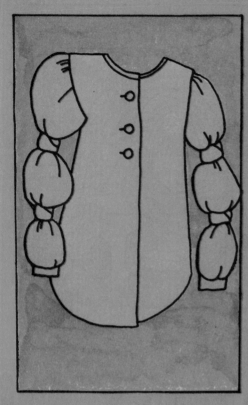

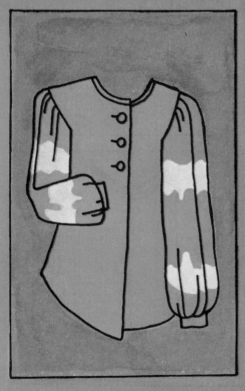

Hannah's mother stirred it around and around. But the blouse didn't turn red . . . it turned orange!

"Dyes are just like paints," Hannah's mother explained. "When you mix two colors together, you get a third color. Red and yellow make orange."

Hannah was very happy because her blouse was even prettier in orange than it had been in yellow.

"But what about those knots in the sleeves?" she was wondering.

After the blouse was dry, she untied the sleeves.

"Oh, how pretty!" she exclaimed.

Where the red dye couldn't touch the sleeves of her blouse because of the knots there were big yellow jagged stripes.

When we dye something at home, it's usually because it's old and we want to give it a new color—like Hannah's old blouse. Most of our clothes are dyed in factories when they're still big pieces of cloth—before they're cut up and made into shirts, pants, and dresses.

Sometimes the thread or yarn is dyed before the cloth is woven together. Then there may be several different-colored threads in one piece of cloth.

Even if you have never dyed a piece of clothing, there is something else that you may dye every year. It's something you eat, not something you wear. Easter eggs!

If you liked this story,
you'll like Thread *in Volume 15*
and Weaving *in Volume 16.*

The Stick That Explodes

One morning almost a hundred years ago, young Alfred Nobel got up from the dinner table and went to his laboratory workshop in the backyard. The next minute he came running back toward the house. Behind him sounded the loudest explosion anyone in the neighborhood had ever heard. Alfred's laboratory disappeared in a burst of flame.

The people of the town were frightened. They were also very angry. They had warned Alfred Nobel against experimenting with explosives. They said if he didn't stop, he would blow up the whole town.

They made him put his new laboratory on a barge. Then they towed the barge out into the middle of a lake. Now, they thought, if there was an explosion, the town would be safe.

Alfred kept on experimenting. He knew that people everywhere needed stronger explosives.

Men were trying to find ways to build railroad tracks over the mountains. They wanted to dig tunnels through the sides of mountains. They wanted to build roads through forests and across rocky plains. They wanted to dig canals for ships to sail through. They needed something to blast away the trees, dirt, and stone. Until now they had used gunpowder, but it just wasn't strong enough.

Some men wanted stronger explosives so that they could make their guns and bombs stronger. This would make their armies more powerful.

Something called *nitroglycerin* had been discovered a few years before, but it was very dangerous. It was an oily liquid that exploded too easily. The slightest shake would sometimes set it

off. People needed an explosive that would not explode until they were ready for it to explode.

Finally Alfred Nobel *did* invent a very strong explosive that could be used easily and more safely. He mixed nitroglycerin with sawdust and shaped it into sticks a little bigger and longer than a cigar. The sticks were wrapped in waxed paper to protect them from the air. He called the sticks *dynamite*.

The dynamite sticks were harmless until they were shaken hard. Then they exploded with great force. With enough dynamite, men could blast a hole through the thickest rock.

People from everywhere in the world bought dynamite. Alfred Nobel became very rich. Dynamite was used in building bridges, roads, and dams. It was used to clear land for homes and cities. It was used to help people live better and more comfortably.

156

But countries also used dynamite to make their armies more powerful. In 1904, in a war between Russia and Japan, dynamite was used in warfare for the first time. Now wars were more dangerous than ever before. Dynamite could kill more people than bullets could.

Alfred Nobel did not want his dynamite to be used to hurt people. He wanted it to be used to help them. Before he died, he decided to give away all his money. Each year some of his money is given to the best scientists and writers and to the person who has done the most to bring peace to the world.

More About Dynamite

The place has been roped off. Sticks of dynamite have been placed in holes drilled in the rock. A man pushes down a handle at the end of a long wire. Electricity runs through the wire and makes the dynamite explode—*bo-oo-om!*

Rocks and dirt fly into the air. When the dust settles, a great hole can be seen in the rock.

A few little sticks of dynamite—how can they do the work of a thousand picks and shovels?

When dynamite is given a hard enough jolt, the chemicals in the small stick turn into a mass of hot gases that push out with tremendous power. The gases

push aside everything that's in their way.

But dynamite is only one kind of explosive. There is another explosive called *gunpowder*. It blows up when it is touched by a spark or a flame.

Anything that burns is explosive if it can be made to burn fast enough—coal gas, gasoline vapor, ether, turpentine.... Tiny explosions of gasoline vapor, set off by sparks from spark plugs, are what make automobiles run.

Black powder—a kind of gunpowder—was the first explosive and the only one known for about 600 years. Many different countries claim to have invented it, but it was probably first used in China. No one knows exactly when it was invented, either. It was first used in guns about 700 years ago.

It was a long time before people thought of using black powder to blast rocks away to make ditches and tunnels.

People used to dig through rock by heating it with fire and then throwing cold water on the rock to make it crack. This was hard, slow work. But 300 years ago in France an engineer named Pierre Paul de Riquet dug a tunnel for a canal by drilling holes in the rock and loading them with black powder. This was the first tunneling with explosives.

Black powder is still used for signal flares, fireworks, time fuses, and special kinds of blasting. But for digging holes and moving rock, engineers use more powerful explosives. After Alfred Nobel invented dynamite, an engineer named Thomas Doane used it in Massachusetts to blast a railroad tunnel through Hoosac Mountain, exploding the dynamite with electricity—the first use of dynamite for tunneling and the first use of electricity to jolt the dynamite into exploding.

Later many other explosives were invented. Most of them contained some form of *nitroglycerin*. An important one is called *TNT*.

A very different kind of explosive, the most powerful of all, was discovered during World War II—the nuclear bomb. This is a very complicated and powerful kind of explosive. This kind of explosive is often made from a rare metal that is dug from the ground—*uranium*. A handful of uranium could make an explosion equal to that made by a whole skyscraper full of TNT.

Nuclear bombs were dropped on the Japanese cities of Hiroshima and Nagasaki during World War II, causing terrible destruction. But peaceful uses for these nuclear explosives are now being found in the United States. Experimenting with nuclear bombs, scientists have dug caves in the desert of New Mexico, as well as a great crater in the Nevada desert.

The Soviet Union and other countries are also experimenting with the peacetime uses of nuclear power. Plans are being made to use nuclear "shovels" to dig new harbors for ships, as well as long tunnels and canals. Perhaps one day, with atomic power, giant icebergs can be broken off the ice fields at the North or South Pole and floated to places where people do not have enough fresh water.